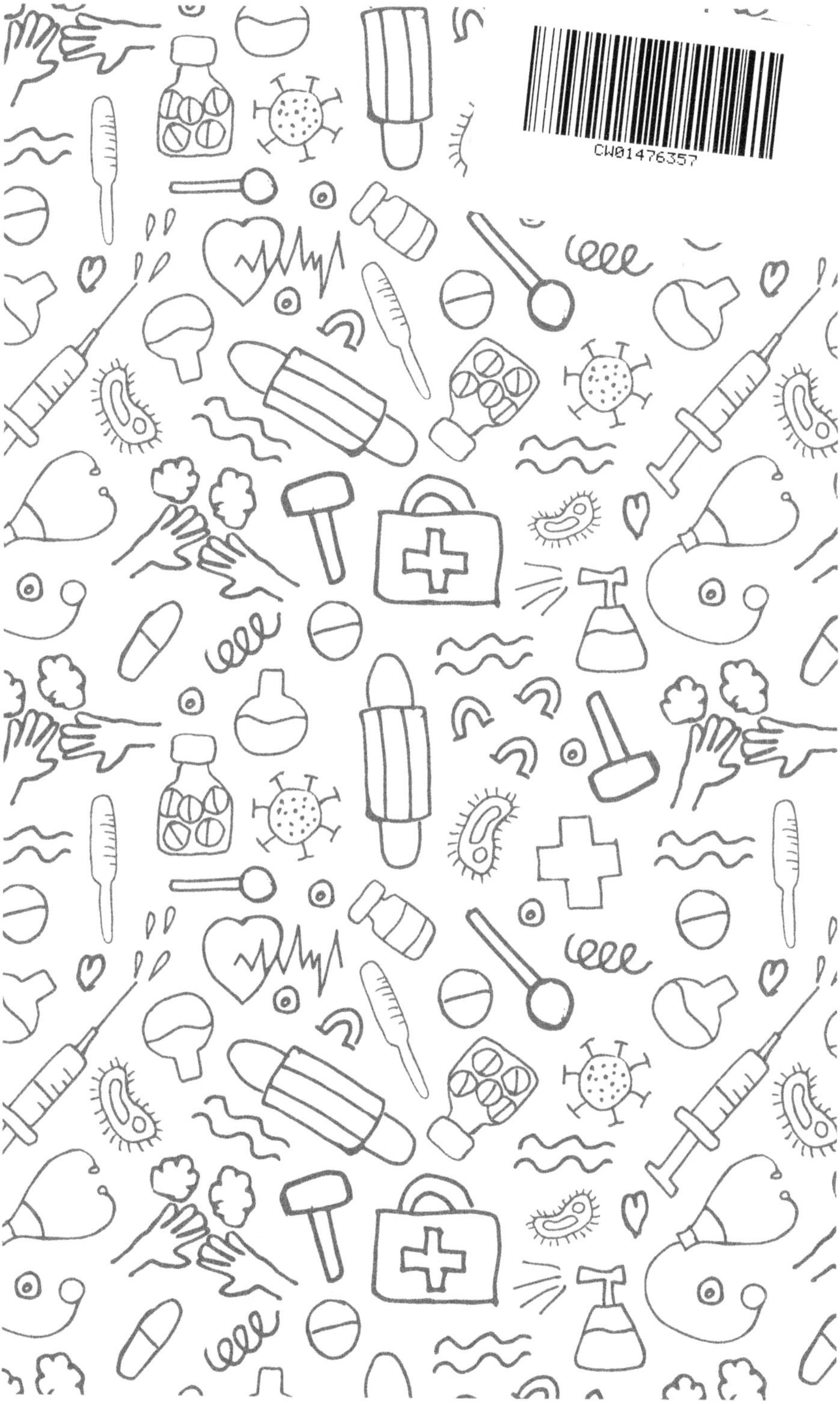

Special Thanks

With all my heart, I want to thank my family for their endless love and support throughout this journey. To my husband, Ryan, and my son, Ravi—your encouragement, patience, and quiet strength have meant more to me than words can express. You were there in every step, every pause, and every breakthrough. This book exists because of your unwavering belief in me. You are my greatest blessings — and this book is a piece of both of you.

Thank you for standing by me,

A NURSE'S GUIDE
TO HEALING THE MIND AND
UPLIFTING THE SOUL

LIGHT
AFTER SHIFT

Zyra Ann Boniel, R.N.

Table of Contents

Table of Contents

WHY I WROTE THIS BOOK

I didn't write this book because I had all the answers - I wrote it because I lived the questions. There was a time when I gave everything to everyone, showing up with a smile while slowly unraveling inside. I was the strong one. The dependable one. But I didn't know how to ask for help - or even name the weight I was carrying.

What I needed wasn't more strength. I needed softness. Support. A reminder that it's okay to fall apart - and possible to heal. So I wrote the book I wish I had. A gentle guide for the givers, the caregivers, the quietly tired souls.

Inside, you won't find perfection. You'll find presence. Simple rituals. Honest words. Space to breathe. And most of all, a reminder: You are not alone. You are not broken. You are already healing.

This is your permission to rest - and come home to yourself.

AUTHOR'S NOTE

This book began as a whisper in my soul during one of the hardest seasons of my life.

As a nurse, I've been trained to care, respond, and show strength in moments of crisis. But over time, I realized I was showing up for everyone - except myself. I knew how to check vitals, respond to emergencies, and document care plans... but I had never been taught how to heal my emotional wounds.

Light After Shift is my offering to every caregiver, every nurse, every strong but silently struggling soul who just needs space to breathe again.

It's part personal journey, part professional insight, and part heartfelt encouragement. I didn't write this book as an expert who has it all figured out.

I wrote it as a fellow human - a nurse, a wife, a mother, and a believer - learning how to come home to myself.

SOURCES OF INSPIRATION

While this book is deeply personal, it was also shaped by the wisdom of others. The following sources and frameworks informed my understanding of stress, burnout, nervous system healing, and emotional care:

Clinical & Scientific Foundations
- The Body Keeps the Score by Dr. Bessel van der Kolk
- Burnout: The Secret to Unlocking the Stress Cycle by Emily & Amelia Nagoski
- Polyvagal Theory by Dr. Stephen Porges
- Mindfulness-Based Stress Reduction (MBSR) by Dr. Jon Kabat-Zinn
- Cognitive Behavioral Therapy (CBT) concepts in mental health nursing
- Studies on nurse burnout and compassion fatigue

Emotional & Spiritual Growth
- Daily prayer and faith-led journaling
- Conversations with fellow nurses, patients, and caregivers
- Inspiration from Scripture and personal spiritual reflection

This book is not a replacement for professional therapy or treatment, but a companion - a soft place to land when life feels heavy. If you are struggling, please seek the help you deserve. Healing is not something you do alone - it's something you receive, step by step, in the presence of grace, support, and truth.

CHAPTER 1
DEPRESSION DOESN'T ALWAYS LOOK SAD

"I laughed with my patients. I made jokes at work.
I posted smiling selfies. And I still cried
in the shower and felt numb during dinner.
Depression didn't show up with tears—
it came disguised as silence."

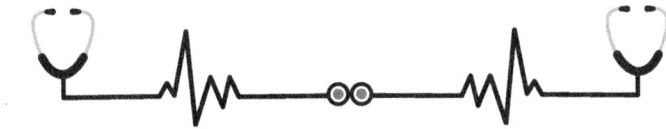

Most people think depression means lying in bed all day, crying, and refusing to talk. But the truth?

Depression often shows up wearing a smile.

It shows up in the nurse who never calls in sick but feels empty inside. In the mom who keeps everyone fed but hasn't eaten a real meal herself. In the man who tells everyone he's "just tired" but can't find the will to get out of the car. In the woman who always checks on others, but no one checks on her.

HIGH-FUNCTIONING DEPRESSION IS REAL

You wake up. You do your job. You smile. You reply to texts. But inside? You feel... off. Disconnected. Not broken, but not whole.

This is called high-functioning depression, and it's real. It's when your outside world keeps spinning, but your inside world is shutting down. It's when you help others heal but forget how to help yourself.

As a nurse, I've seen patients with broken bones receive immediate attention.

But emotional pain?

It's often dismissed or misunderstood - even by ourselves.

THE 5 INVISIBLE SIGNS OF HIDDEN DEPRESSION

You might not realize you're experiencing early signs of depression.

Here are five subtle red flags:

1. You feel exhausted, even after sleeping.
   - Not physically tired - soul tired.

2. You lose interest in the little things you used to enjoy.
   - Music. Coffee. Sunsets. They're... dull.

3. You zone out or feel like life is on autopilot.
   - You're present - but not really there.

4. You feel guilty for no clear reason.
   - Especially when you're doing "nothing." Rest feels wrong.

5. You're overwhelmed by simple decisions.
   - What to wear. What to eat. Everything feels like too much.

Sound familiar?

YOU ARE NOT WEAK - YOU'RE CARRYING TOO MUCH

Let's get one thing clear: Depression is not weakness. It's not laziness. It's not selfishness.

It's a sign that your nervous system is overworked, your heart is overloaded, and your mind is asking for help.

Would you judge a patient who collapsed from a heart attack?

Would you blame a diabetic for their blood sugar drop?
Of course not.

So why do we judge ourselves for emotional burnout or sadness?

WHAT DEPRESSION IS TRYING TO TELL YOU

Depression is the body and soul saying:

- "I need rest, not more pressure."

- "I need love, not perfection."

- "I need connection, not comparison."

- "I need safety, not silence."

When you listen to these whispers early, you can start healing before the cracks become fractures.

TRY THIS TODAY: THE 2-MINUTE BODY SCAN

Right now, pause.
Place one hand on your heart.
Close your eyes.
Take a deep breath in for 4 seconds... hold...
and exhale slowly.

Now ask yourself, gently:

- How am I, really?
- Where in my body do I feel tension?
- What is one kind thing I can do for myself today?

Sometimes the bravest thing we can do is simply check-in.

REFLECTION QUESTIONS:

- When was the last time I felt truly like myself?

- What daily habits have changed in me lately?

- Who can I talk to about how I feel—without fear of judgment?

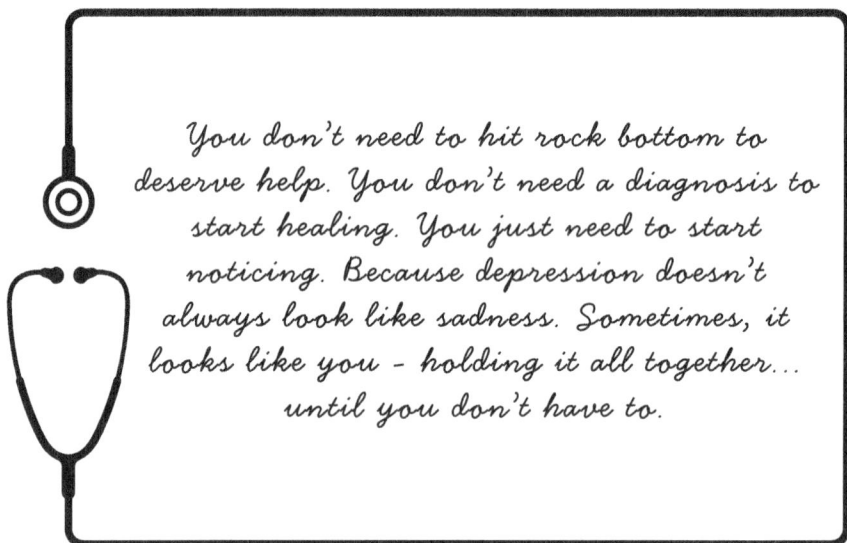

You don't need to hit rock bottom to deserve help. You don't need a diagnosis to start healing. You just need to start noticing. Because depression doesn't always look like sadness. Sometimes, it looks like you - holding it all together... until you don't have to.

CHAPTER 2
THE SCIENCE OF A HEAVY MIND

"When your mind is heavy, even brushing your teeth feels like climbing a mountain. It's not in your head - it's in your nervous system, your hormones, your chemistry. Depression isn't imagined. It's real, and it's biological."

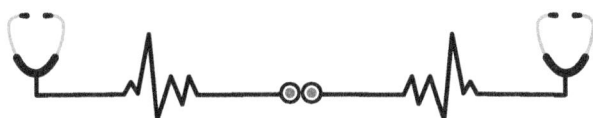

WHY AM I LIKE THIS?
(THE BRAIN'S HONEST ANSWER)

If you've ever asked yourself,

"Why can't I just snap out of it?"
"What's wrong with me?"
"Why do I feel like this even when my life looks okay?"

You're not alone - and you're not broken.
The truth is: depression and mental fatigue have biological roots. Understanding what's happening in your brain and body is the first step toward healing without shame.

DEPRESSION AND THE BRAIN: A QUICK NURSE'S BREAKDOWN

Let's talk science - but make it simple.

- **Serotonin & Dopamine: The Feel-Good Messengers**

When you're mentally well, your brain releases a healthy balance of serotonin (mood stabilizer) and dopamine (pleasure/reward).

When you're burned out, overwhelmed, or depressed, those levels can drop, making it harder to feel joy, focus, or motivation.

- **Cortisol: The Stress Alarm Bell**

Chronic stress (like long shifts, emotional trauma, or life pressure) keeps your cortisol levels high. This drains your body, disrupts sleep, and increases anxiety.

- **Your Nervous System: Always on Alert**

Your body has two modes:

- Fight or flight (sympathetic nervous system)

- Rest and heal (parasympathetic nervous system)

Depression and anxiety often mean your body is stuck in "alert mode" and forgets how to truly rest.

BURNOUT VS DEPRESSION: WHAT'S THE DIFFERENCE

Burnout is emotional and physical exhaustion caused by prolonged stress.

Depression is a clinical mood disorder that affects your thoughts, behavior, and body.

But the symptoms overlap - and one can lead to the other if untreated.

Shared Symptoms:
- Numbness or detachment
- Sleep issues
- Low motivation
- Feeling overwhelmed
- Withdrawal from others

Difference:
Burnout improves with rest.
Depression lingers, even with time off.
If you're unsure which you're facing, it's okay.
What matters is noticing and taking action before it deepens.

TRAUMA AND THE NURSE BRAIN

Let's not ignore this: nurses are exposed to trauma every day.

Grief. Code blues. Emotional pressure. Death. Family dynamics. Pandemic scars. Compassion fatigue.

When your brain experiences vicarious trauma (absorbing others' pain), it rewires itself for survival, not joy. That's why you might feel "off" even if nothing big happened to you.

The brain remembers what the soul can't process in the moment.

YOU'RE NOT OVERREACTING YOU'RE OVERFLOWING

When people say, "You're just being sensitive," Or, "You're so dramatic," Or worse - "You have nothing to be sad about..."

Remember:
Your nervous system doesn't care if your stress is "big" or "small."

It only knows when it's overwhelmed.

And your brain responds by shutting down joy to conserve energy.

This is not a weakness. This is survival.

TRY THIS TODAY: THE BRAIN RESET BREATH

Set a timer for 2 minutes.

Sit or lie down.

Inhale for 4 seconds, hold for 4, exhale for 6.

Repeat this slow breath pattern while saying silently: "I am safe. I am not in danger. I am allowed to rest."

This tells your nervous system: we're not in crisis anymore.

It's a signal that allows your body to shift from surviving to healing.

REFLECTION QUESTIONS:

- Where do I feel pressure in my life right now?

- What stress am I carrying that I've never said out loud?

- If my brain could speak, what would it say it needs?

You're not losing your mind.
Your mind is tired.
And just like a sprained ankle needs rest,
a heavy brain needs care.
Let's give it that care -
one gentle shift at a time.

CHAPTER 3
MICRO-MOMENTS THAT HEAL

"Healing doesn't have to be a grand gesture.
Sometimes it's the way you sit in the sunlight
for two minutes. The way you whisper
'I'm doing my best' between deep breaths."

HEALING IS IN THE SMALLEST THINGS

In nursing, we often think healing means intervention: IV drips, surgeries, medication, or crisis stabilization. But mental health healing? It begins much smaller.

It begins in micro-moments.
Moments so simple, we often overlook them.
Moments that whisper to your nervous system:

You're safe now. You can breathe. You don't need a vacation. You need a pause. You need permission. You need presence.

WHAT ARE MICRO-HEALING MOMENTS?

They're small shifts that anchor your brain back to the present. They calm the fight-or-flight response and allow your body to feel grounded - even if just for seconds. They're not dramatic. But they are powerful.

Examples:
- Standing barefoot on the ground for one minute
- Looking up at the sky and noticing the color
- Drinking water without multitasking
- Placing your hand over your heart and saying "I'm here"
- Lighting a candle at the end of your shift as a ritual of release
- Washing your face slowly, as an act of care - not just routine

These don't fix everything. But they interrupt the spiral. And that's where healing begins.

FROM NURSE MODE
TO HUMAN MODE

As nurses, we're trained to keep going. Even on empty. Even in chaos. Even when it hurts. But you are not just a nurse. You are human. And your healing doesn't require permission from your charting list, unit manager, or schedule.

Start by inserting 5-second pauses into your day.

Here's how:
- Before walking into a patient's room, pause and feel your feet on the floor.
- After washing your hands, take one slow, intentional breath.
- When you clock out, whisper "Today is done. I did my best."

These small moments reclaim your humanity.

TRY THIS TODAY: CREATE A MICRO-HEALING MENU

Write down 5 simple things you can do in less than 3 minutes that make you feel calm, cared for, or connected.

Example Menu:

- Step outside and look at the trees
- Stretch your arms and breathe for 60 seconds
- Write one line in a journal: "Today I feel..."
- Play a calming song and close your eyes
- Look in the mirror and smile - gently

Tape your list somewhere visible: your bathroom mirror, your locker, or your car dashboard.

In moments of overwhelm, choose one.
It may not fix the day - but it might save the hour.

WHY IT WORKS
(NURSE SCIENCE)

Micro-moments activate your parasympathetic nervous system.

This slows your heart rate, regulates your breath, and decreases cortisol.

Over time, these tiny practices retrain your brain to come back to safety more easily.

They don't replace therapy or medication.
But they're the daily vitamins your soul needs.

REFLECTION QUESTIONS:

- What small habit have I dropped that once made me feel good?

- When was the last time I felt peaceful - even for a moment?

- Can I gift myself just 3 minutes a day to slow down?

This chapter isn't about fixing yourself.

It's about remembering you are already
whole - just exhausted.

And in the quietest, smallest moments...
healing begins.

CHAPTER 4
BECOMING YOUR OWN CAREGIVER

"You care for everyone else.
But who cares for you?
What if... it could be you?"

THE NURSE
WHO FORGOT HERSELF

It's strange, isn't it? We show up for strangers with every ounce of our being. We monitor vitals, offer words of comfort, and anticipate pain before it even surfaces. We advocate. We educate. We soothe. But when it's our pain?

We ignore it. We minimize it. We numb it. We say, "I'm fine," while quietly breaking.

Because we were never taught how to care for ourselves with the same urgency, compassion, and commitment we give others. It's time to change that.

THE CARE PLAN: YOU

What if you were your patient?

What if you created a personal care plan like you do for others - charting needs, goals, interventions, and outcomes?

What if you spoke to yourself the way you speak to a patient who's hurting?

"You're doing great. Let's take this one breath at a time."

"I'm not here to judge you - I'm here to help you."

"You are not alone."

This chapter is your reminder that you are worthy of the care you give so freely.

3 PILLARS OF SELF-CARE
(THAT GO BEYOND BUBBLE BATHS)

Forget the fluffy version of self-care. Let's get real. True self-care - especially when preventing depression - is grounded in honesty, boundaries, and intentional healing.

1. Compassion Over Criticism

Replace internal self-talk like:
- "Why can't I just get it together?"
- "I'm so lazy."
- "Other people have it worse."

With:
- "I'm doing the best I can with what I have."
- "This is hard, and I'm allowed to feel it."
- "I am not weak for needing rest."

Self-compassion isn't coddling - it's rewiring your nervous system to feel safe with yourself.

2. Boundaries Are Medicine

Saying "no" is a prescription. So is stepping away from toxic conversations, overcommitting, and pretending you're okay when you're not.

Boundaries create emotional oxygen. Without them, you suffocate in silent resentment.

3. Daily Rituals of Check-In

Just like we assess patients on rounds, we must assess ourselves.

Ask daily:

- What do I need today: Rest, movement, connection, quiet?

- What emotion is loudest in me right now?

- What can I let go of today - even temporarily?

TRY THIS TODAY:
WRITE YOUR OWN CARE PLAN

Create a basic care plan... for you.

Nursing Diagnosis (Emotional):
Impaired emotional well-being related to prolonged stress, as evidenced by fatigue, irritability, and loss of joy.

Goal:
To feel supported, grounded, and more connected to self within 14 days.

Interventions:
- 10-minute quiet time before bed
- Say "no" once this week without guilt
- Call a friend just to talk
- Journal feelings for 5 minutes daily
- Practice one breathwork session per shift

Outcome Criteria:
- Improved sleep
- Less self-criticism
- Increased awareness of needs
- Sense of control returning

Stick this in your journal or phone. Review it weekly. Adjust as needed. You're the nurse, and you're the patient.

REFLECTION QUESTIONS:

- What kind of support do I offer others that I withhold from myself?

- What's one small thing I can do this week that says "I matter"?

- Where in my life do I need to start setting boundaries?

You have spent years keeping others alive.
Let's not forget to keep ourselves alive,
too - not just physically, but emotionally,
spiritually, mentally.
Become the caregiver you've always
needed... starting now.

CHAPTER 5
RESETTING THE NERVOUS SYSTEM

"Your body isn't betraying you.
It's just tired of living in survival mode."

THE SYSTEM THAT KEEPS YOU ALIVE... AND EXHAUSTED

We talk about the heart. We talk about the brain. But what about the nervous system - the silent command center of everything you feel, do, and remember?

Your nervous system is the invisible thread between your mind and body. When it's balanced, you feel clear, connected, calm. When it's overactivated for too long, you feel anxious, numb, reactive - or just plain exhausted. And here's the truth: most of us, especially nurses, live in survival mode far too often.

FIGHT, FLIGHT, FREEZE... OR FAWN

When stress hits, your body shifts into one of four responses:

- Fight: You get irritable, angry, or defensive.
- Flight: You avoid, distract, or keep busy to escape feelings.
- Freeze: You shut down, go numb, or feel stuck or paralyzed.
- Fawn: You people - please, over-apologize, or lose your own needs to stay safe.

Sound familiar?

These responses aren't wrong. They're protective. They helped you survive trauma, pressure, grief, and chaos.

But healing happens when we move out of survival mode - and into safety.

THE PARASYMPATHETIC POWER

The parasympathetic nervous system is your "rest and digest" state.

It's where real healing, connection, and joy can finally happen.

But to activate it, you must give your body cues that you are no longer in danger.

This doesn't require hours of meditation or silence. It requires presence. Intention. Consistency.

SIMPLE WAYS TO RESET YOUR NERVOUS SYSTEM

You don't need a retreat. You need rituals.

Here are small, nurse-approved tools to reset and re-regulate:

1. Grounding Through the Senses

- Hold something warm (a mug of tea or warm compress)
- Light a candle and notice the flame for 30 seconds
- Stand barefoot on the ground or floor
- Slowly rub lotion into your hands, focusing on the texture and smell

2. Patterned Breathing

Use the 4-7-8 method:

- Inhale for 4 seconds
- Hold for 7 seconds
- Exhale slowly for 8 seconds
- Repeat 4 cycles. It sends a "calm" signal to your vagus nerve.

3. **Humming or Singing**

Yes, really.

Humming activates the vagus nerve, which signals your body to relax. Try humming to your favorite song - loudly, gently, awkwardly - it all works.

4. **Cold Splash Technique**

Splash cold water on your face or place a cool towel across your cheeks and eyes.

This activates the "dive reflex," which calms your heart rate and resets your stress response.

CREATE A DAILY RESET RITUAL

Choose one calming tool to practice every day for 5 minutes.

Make it part of your post-shift routine, your lunch break, or your pre-bed wind-down.

Example Ritual:

- Light a candle
- Take 5 deep breaths with your hand on your heart
- Journal one sentence: "Right now, I feel..."
- Drink something warm slowly
- Thank your body for carrying you today

Healing the nervous system isn't about doing it perfectly.
It's about showing up - gently, consistently, and lovingly.

TRY THIS TODAY: YOUR NERVOUS SYSTEM RESET

Choose one ritual and set a reminder to do it once a day for the next 3 days.

Notice any small shift: less tension in your shoulders, better sleep, fewer racing thoughts.

Healing starts with regulation - not perfection.

REFLECTION QUESTIONS:

- When do I feel most tense during the day?

- What environment or routine helps me feel safe?

- What signal does my body give me when I've ignored stress for too long?

Your nervous system is not your enemy.
It's been protecting you. But now, it's safe
to rest. It's safe to slow down.
And with each breath, you're telling your
body: 'You made it. You can let go.'

CHAPTER 6

THE POWER OF THOUGHT MEDICINE

"Your thoughts are not just words in your mind.
They are instructions to your nervous system.
What you think, you feel.
What you believe, you become."

THE INNER VOICE
THAT SHAPES YOUR WORLD

Let's be honest. If someone spoke to us the way we speak to ourselves... we'd call it emotional abuse. "You're not doing enough." "You should be stronger by now." "Everyone else seems okay - why can't you be?" "You're such a burden." "You're failing."

These are not harmless thoughts. They are wounds in disguise. Our inner voice becomes the soundtrack of our nervous system. If the tune is full of fear, guilt, and shame - your body responds with tension, fatigue, and sadness. But here's the powerful truth: You can change the channel.

53

COGNITIVE REFRAMING: THE NURSE'S MENTAL SHIFT

In nursing, we reframe all the time.

- A wound isn't "ugly" - it's healing.
- A patient isn't "difficult" - they're scared or in pain.
- A code isn't just chaos - it's a coordinated dance of urgency and teamwork.

We give things new meaning so we can act with clarity and compassion.

You can do the same for your thoughts.

Cognitive reframing is the process of gently questioning, challenging, and transforming negative thought patterns into ones that support healing and truth.

FROM THOUGHT TRAPS TO HEALING THOUGHTS

Here's how to spot a "thought trap" - and what to reframe it into:

Thought Trap	Healing Reframe
"I'm not good enough."	"I am doing the best I can with what I have."
"I'm broken."	"I am healing."
"I can't handle this."	"This is hard, but I don't have to do it all at once."
"I'm a burden."	"I am allowed to ask for help."
"I'm failing."	"I am learning to be human, not perfect."

Healing doesn't mean you never have negative thoughts. It means you stop believing every single one of them.

THE SCIENCE OF THOUGHT & DEPRESSION

Your thoughts impact your brain chemistry.

Negative thinking patterns increase cortisol and suppress dopamine and serotonin - deepening fatigue, anxiety, and sadness.

Positive, grounded thoughts (especially when practiced regularly) help rewire neural pathways, increasing resilience and emotional regulation.

You're retraining your brain when you shift your inner dialogue.

TRY THIS TODAY: THE THOUGHT AUDIT

Take a few minutes and write down 3 thoughts that keep repeating in your mind - especially during stress or sadness.

Now ask:

- Is this thought true?
- Where did I learn this?
- What is a more helpful version of this thought?

Then reframe it. Write the new version on a sticky note, your phone, or your mirror.

Let it guide you.

Let it remind you: your thoughts are not your enemy - they're your responsibility.

AFFIRMATIONS FOR THE HEALING NURSE

You don't have to believe these fully yet - just speak them out loud or write them down.

"I am allowed to rest without guilt."

"I deserve the same care I give to others."

"I am not alone in this journey."

"Healing is not linear - and I am still healing."

"I trust that light is returning to me."

Words are medicine.

Use them wisely, often, and kindly.

REFLECTION QUESTIONS:

- What old belief do I need to release to heal?

- What do I say to others that I rarely say to myself?

- If I spoke to myself like a patient, what would I say today?

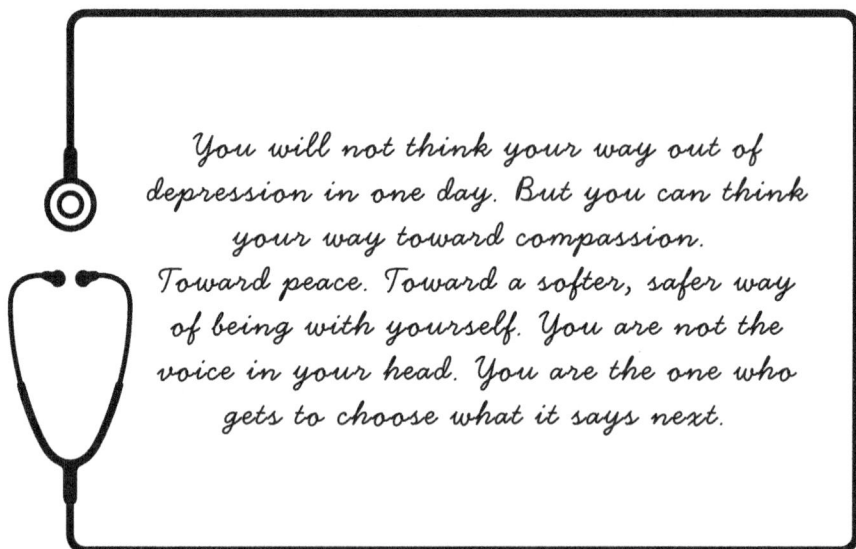

You will not think your way out of depression in one day. But you can think your way toward compassion. Toward peace. Toward a softer, safer way of being with yourself. You are not the voice in your head. You are the one who gets to choose what it says next.

CHAPTER 7
MOVEMENT AS MEDICINE

"Your body remembers everything your mind tries to forget. Let it move. Let it release. Let it heal."

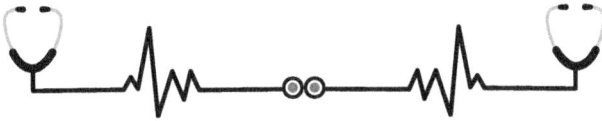

THE STILLNESS THAT HURTS

Depression has a way of making the body still. Not restful still - paralyzed still. It drains energy, motivation, and will. Even standing up can feel like a battle.

But here's something we often forget:
The body carries unprocessed emotions.
It holds tension in the shoulders, trauma in the chest, and fear in the gut. And when we don't move, we don't release. We stay stuck.

The good news?

You don't need a gym membership, fancy clothes, or even motivation. You need one thing: gentle permission to move again.

WHY MOVEMENT HEALS THE MIND

Movement isn't just for muscles.

It directly affects your brain and nervous system.

Here's how it helps:

- Boosts dopamine + serotonin - improves mood
- Reduces cortisol - lowers stress
- Activates the vagus nerve - promotes calm
- Breaks the freeze response - and gets you unstuck
- Restores trust in the body — strengthens mind-body connection

It's not about burning calories.
It's about burning through emotional fog.

THE MOVEMENT MYTH: YOU DON'T HAVE TO GO HARD

When we think "exercise," we picture loud music, sweat, pushing limits.

But healing movement is the opposite.

It's gentle, mindful, and nurturing.

If you're burned out, you don't need a workout. You need a reunion with your body.

TYPES OF HEALING MOVEMENT

Here are small ways to reintroduce movement into your healing:

1. Stretching With Intention

Take 5 minutes to stretch your arms, neck, shoulders, and back. Breathe deeply with each stretch. Feel where you hold tension - and gently let go.

2. Walking Without a Goal

No steps to track. No speed is required. Just movement and breath. Walk slowly around the block or even inside your home. Be present.

3. Somatic Shaking

Stand with knees soft. Shake your arms, shoulders, and hips for 1–2 minutes. Let your body release stress like animals do after trauma. (It works!)

4. Yoga for Recovery

Restorative or trauma-informed yoga reconnects breath and body. No performance. Just healing.

5. Dance Therapy

Put on music and let your body move - no rules, no choreography. Just freedom. Let your inner child play.

TRY THIS TODAY: ONE SONG, ONE MOVEMENT

Pick one slow, gentle song.

Stand or sit. Close your eyes.

Start moving your hands, and your shoulders, or sway side to side.

No pressure. Just presence.

When the song ends, check-in:

- How do I feel now?
- What shifted?

This is your healing practice - just 3 minutes a day.

MOVEMENT DOESN'T FIX EVERYTHING - BUT IT UNLOCKS SOMETHING

Sometimes, grief is stored in the hips.

Anger hides in the jaw.

Fear tenses the belly.

Movement is how we let the body tell its side of the story.

REFLECTION QUESTIONS:

- What is one part of my body that feels tense or heavy right now?

- When was the last time I moved without purpose - just for pleasure or release?

- What kind of movement feels nourishing to me?

You do not have to be strong.
You do not have to be fast.
You just have to begin.
Because movement is medicine.
And you, dear nurse, deserve to heal.

CHAPTER 8
LIGHT, SLEEP, AND NOURISHMENT

*"Healing isn't just emotional—it's biological.
Your body needs light. It needs rest. It needs fuel.
You're not just tired—you're undernourished
in soul and system."*

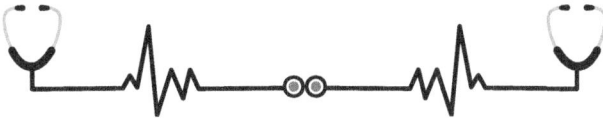

THE PHYSICAL FOUNDATION OF MENTAL HEALTH

You can't outthink a tired body. You can't meditate your way out of hormone imbalances, sleep debt, or vitamin deficiencies. Mental wellness begins in the body. Your mood is connected to your biology more than we like to admit. As nurses, we see this in our patients. But when was the last time we assessed our baseline?

- Are we sleeping deeply?
- Are we getting natural light?
- Are we eating real meals - or surviving on caffeine and vending machines?

When these basics are missing, so is our peace.

LET THERE BE LIGHT

Light is not just visual - it's hormonal.

Sunlight regulates your circadian rhythm, improves serotonin production, and reduces depressive symptoms.

Try this:

- Within 30 minutes of waking, step outside - even for 5 minutes

- Let natural light hit your face (no sunglasses)

- On night shifts, use a daylight lamp in the morning to reset your rhythm

Light tells your brain,
"You're alive. You're safe. You're part of this world."

SLEEP:
THE INVISIBLE MEDICINE

You might be used to running for 5 hours.
You might call it strength. But your body
calls it distress. Poor sleep increases anxiety,
irritability, inflammation, and depression.

How to improve sleep, even with odd shifts:

- Create a "wind-down ritual" before bed
(music, tea, dim lights)

- Keep your bedroom cool, dark, and screen-
free

- Use a white noise machine to reduce
sudden wake-ups

- Sleep in consistent blocks when possible -
even if not at night

Don't just "crash" - prepare for sleep. Make it
sacred.

TRY THIS TODAY: THE "DAILY RESET TRIO

Check-in with these three elements:

- **Did I get natural light today?**

- **Did I sleep at least 6 hours?**

- **Did I eat something nourishing - not just fast fuel**?

If the answer is no, that's your gentle nudge.

Start small. Even one improvement makes a difference.

REFLECTION QUESTIONS:

- What physical need have I ignored lately?

- What food, light, or sleep habits do I want to improve this week?

- Do I treat my body as something sacred... or something to push?

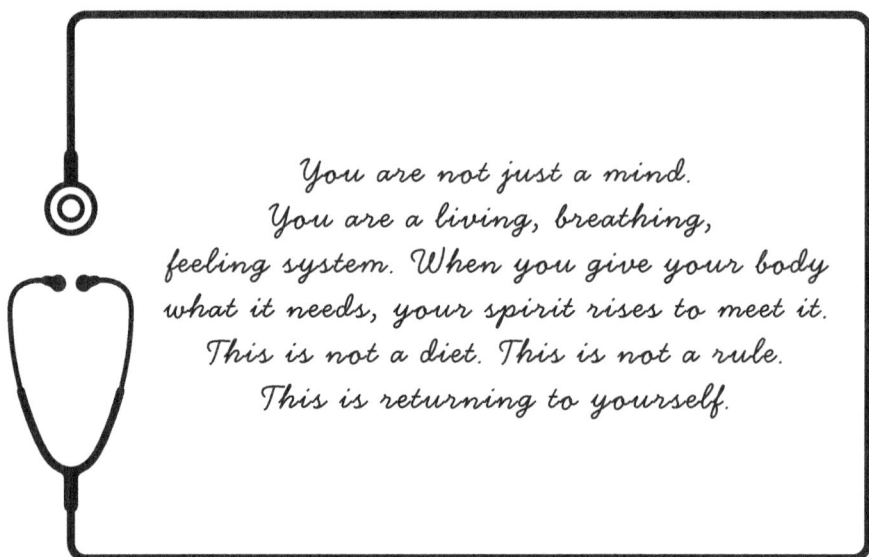

You are not just a mind.
You are a living, breathing,
feeling system. When you give your body
what it needs, your spirit rises to meet it.
This is not a diet. This is not a rule.
This is returning to yourself.

CHAPTER 9
BUILDING YOUR SUPPORT TEAM

"You don't have to do this alone.
Healing may be personal, but it was
never meant to be solitary."

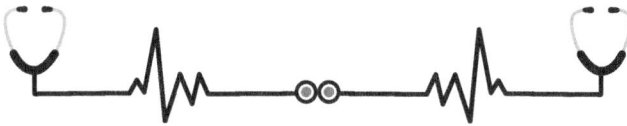

THE MYTH OF THE STRONG ONE

As nurses, caregivers, and healers, we're often seen as the strong ones. The dependable ones. The ones who keep it together. And we start to believe the myth:

"I should be able to handle this by myself."
"I don't want to be a burden."
"No one has time for my problems."
"Everyone else seems fine."

But here's the truth: even the strongest need someone to lean on. Isolation feeds depression. Connection nourishes healing.

WHY WE STRUGGLE TO ASK FOR HELP

You might feel guilt.
You might fear judgment.
You might have learned early that it's safer to be silent.

But staying silent doesn't protect you.
It isolates you.

Mental health isn't just about what's happening inside - it's about what's available outside.

You need a team. Not just in the workplace - but in life.

THE 3 TYPES OF PEOPLE YOU NEED IN YOUR HEALING CIRCLE

Think of these as your emotional care team - the people who see the real you, love you through it, and hold space for healing.

1. The Listener
They won't try to fix you. They'll just sit with you. This person says, "Tell me everything," and means it.

2. The Truth-Teller
They'll call you out - with love. They won't let you isolate, disappear, or believe your worst thoughts. They remind you of your worth when you forget it.

3. The Lifter
They make you laugh. They send the memes. They bring light when things feel heavy.
Sometimes, they don't say anything deep - they just remind you joy still exists.

YOU DESERVE
TO BE HELD, TOO

You've held hands through tears.
You've comforted grieving families.
You've shown up for so many.

You deserve that same level of care.

Even one safe person can change everything.
Whether it's a therapist, a friend, a spiritual
guide, or a fellow nurse who "gets it."

Let them in.
Let them know you're not okay.
Let them love you anyway.

WHEN YOU DON'T HAVE SUPPORT YET...

Sometimes, we truly feel like we have no one. In those moments:

- Start with a journal.
- Try anonymous online support groups or hotlines.
- Reach out to a therapist - even just for a consultation.
- Listen to podcasts or books where you feel seen.
- Remind yourself: you're not the only one.

You are never as alone as you think.

REFLECTION QUESTIONS:

- Who do I feel safest with right now?

- What's stopping me from reaching out for help?

- What kind of support do I need - and am I willing to receive it?

Healing doesn't happen in isolation.
It happens in connection, conversation,
and compassion. You're not meant to
carry this alone. You never were.
This is your permission to learn.
To speak. To be held.

CHAPTER 10

HOPE IS A DAILY HABIT

*"Hope isn't something you find.
It's something you choose—again and again,
until it becomes part of you."*

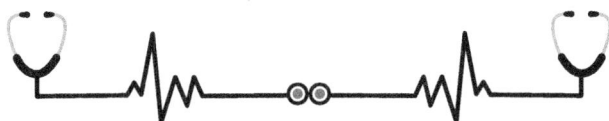

NOT A FEELING - A PRACTICE

Some days, hope feels like a faraway dream. Other days, it feels like a whisper in your chest: "Maybe... things could get better." What if hope wasn't just a feeling that visited you on good days? What if it was a habit you could build? Hope doesn't always roar. Sometimes, it simply shows up in your choices.

- Getting out of bed when it's hard
- Sending the message that says, "I need to talk"
- Drinking water when you feel empty
- Writing down one thing you're grateful for, even if it's just breathing

These are acts of hope.

THE PHYSIOLOGY OF HOPE

Yes, even hope has a science.

Research shows that hopeful thinking activates the brain's reward system - boosting dopamine and encouraging action, even in tough times. And unlike blind optimism, hope isn't denial.

Hope says:

"This is hard - and I still believe in the possibility of peace."

Your nervous system responds to this belief with motivation, safety, and openness.

Hope is healing.

HOW TO PRACTICE HOPE DAILY

Let's make hope practical - not poetic.

Here are simple ways to build a habit of hope, one day at a time:

1. The Morning Light Practice
Each morning, before checking your phone:
- Step outside or near a window
- Take 3 deep breaths
- Whisper or write: "I am open to light today."

Even if your heart doesn't feel it - your brain will begin to.

2. The Gratitude Reframe
Each night, write down:
- One thing that brought you comfort
- One small win (even if it's "I made it through")
- One thing you hope for tomorrow

Gratitude doesn't ignore the dark - it reminds you the light still exists.

3. Keep a "Hope File"

This is a folder, notebook, or note in your phone:

- Screenshots of kind messages
- Photos that make you smile
- Quotes or affirmations that move you
- Notes to yourself from better days

Read it when you forget who you are.
Let it be your mirror on days when your reflection feels blurred.

TRY THIS TODAY: A 5-MINUTE HOPE RITUAL

Right now:

- Put your hand over your heart
- Breathe in slowly and say: "I am still here."
- Think of one thing you're looking forward to - even if small (a cup of tea, a phone call, a warm shower)
- Write it down. That's your anchor today.

Hope lives in your awareness of the present and your belief in what's ahead.

WHEN YOU CAN'T FIND HOPE

If you've searched and come up empty, let this be your reminder:

- You're not weak. You're tired.
- Hope will return. It always does.
- Until then, let others hold it for you.

Sometimes, just reading this chapter is proof of your hope. You picked up this book. You're here. You're still trying. And that's enough.

REFLECTION QUESTIONS:

- What's one thing I'm grateful for right now?

- What's one thing I hope for, even if I'm scared to say it?

- How can I create a 5-minute ritual of hope this week?

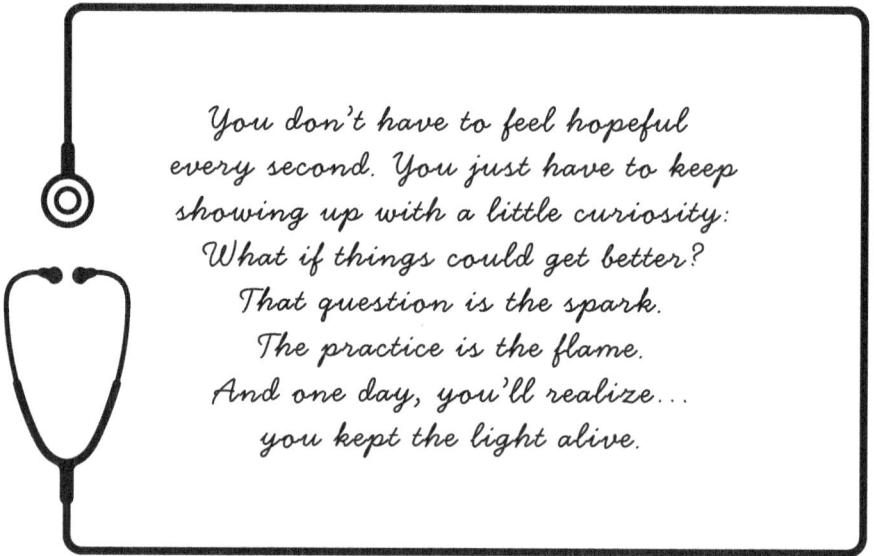

You don't have to feel hopeful
every second. You just have to keep
showing up with a little curiosity:
What if things could get better?
That question is the spark.
The practice is the flame.
And one day, you'll realize...
you kept the light alive.

CHAPTER 11
14-DAY MENTAL WELLNESS RESET

*"You don't have to change your whole life overnight.
You just need to take one small step today -
then another tomorrow."*

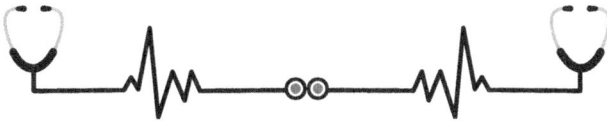

WHY A RESET -
NOT A REINVENTION

Healing isn't about flipping a switch. It's about gently recalibrating your life one moment at a time. This 14-day reset is designed for real people with real schedules - nurses, caregivers, parents, night-shift warriors, and the emotionally exhausted.

No pressure. No perfection. Each day includes one small act of care for your mind, body, and spirit. You don't have to do them all.

Just do something.

HOW IT WORKS

- Each day has one small action focused on mind, body, or spirit

- All activities can be done in 10 minutes or less

- You can start on any day of the week

- Miss a day? That's okay. Pick up where you left off.

Let this reset be your return home to yourself.

14-DAY MENTAL WELLNESS RESET

Day 1: Ground Yourself

Sit outside or near a window. Take 5 slow breaths. Feel your feet on the ground. Repeat silently: "I am here. I am safe. I am allowed to be still."

Day 2: Light Intake

Get at least 10 minutes of sunlight today - morning is best. Let your face, hands, and body receive it without distraction.

Day 3: Digital Detox (Mini)

For one hour, turn off notifications. Be present with whatever you're doing - without checking your phone. Feel the difference in your mind.

Day 4: Write It Out

Journal one page answering this: "What have I been carrying lately that I want to release?"

Day 5: Move Gently

Stretch, dance, walk, or shake for 5 minutes. Let your body move in any way that feels natural. This is not for fitness. This is for freedom.

Day 6: Speak Kindly to Yourself

Look in the mirror and say:
"I am doing my best. I am proud of myself for trying." Write down one affirmation to repeat throughout the day.

Day 7: Reconnect with Someone

Text or call someone you trust. You don't need to explain everything - just say, "Thinking of you."

Day 8: Nourish with Intention

Eat one meal today with full presence.
No multitasking. Just taste, chew, and breathe.
Let food be medicine.

Day 9: Declutter Your Space (or Mind)

Choose one small area - a drawer, a bag,
your notes app. Clear something physical or
emotional. Let it feel like a fresh start.

Day 10: Practice "Just Being"

Sit or lie down and simply exist. No agenda.
No goals. No expectations. Let yourself be a
human, not a task list.

Day 11: Ask for Help (Even Small Help)

Let someone support you - carry a bag,
make a decision, and listen. Practice receiving.
You don't always have to carry it alone.

Day 12: Return to Nature

Sit outside, take a walk, or open a window and listen to the sounds. Look at the sky, the trees, a plant. Let the earth remind you: healing is slow - and beautiful.

Day 13: Sleep Reset

Go to bed 30 minutes earlier. Make your space peaceful - dim lights, soothing sounds, no screens. Let your body receive real rest.

Day 14: Reflect & Celebrate

Write down 3 shifts you've felt during this reset. Celebrate your consistency, not perfection. End with this statement: "I am healing. I am whole. I am worthy of peace."

REFLECTION QUESTIONS:

- Which day's practice felt most natural to me?

- Which was most difficult - and why?

- How can I carry one of these practices into my daily life?

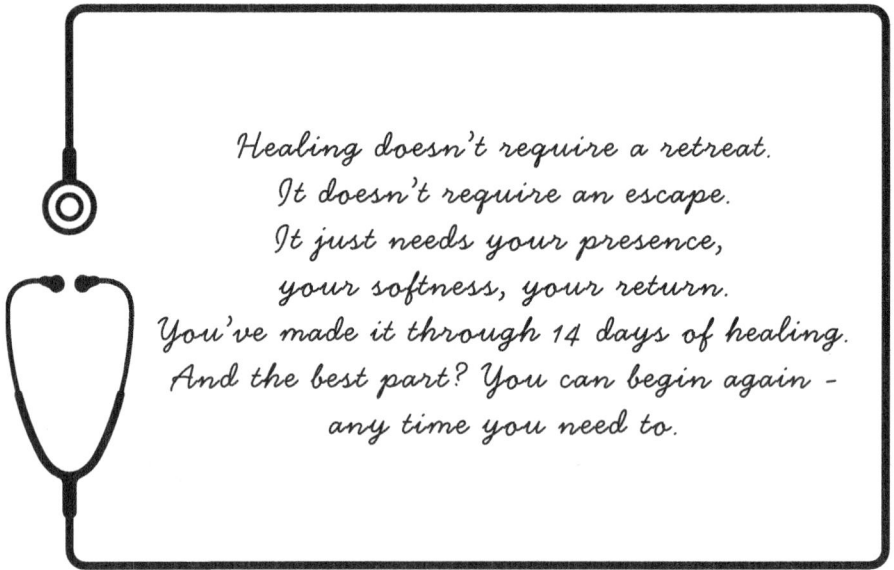

Healing doesn't require a retreat.
It doesn't require an escape.
It just needs your presence,
your softness, your return.
You've made it through 14 days of healing.
And the best part? You can begin again -
any time you need to.

CHAPTER 12
THE SHIFT IN ME
(FINAL THOUGHTS)

*"The greatest shift wasn't in my schedule.
It wasn't in my environment.
It was in how I chose to see myself - no longer
as someone broken... but someone becoming."*

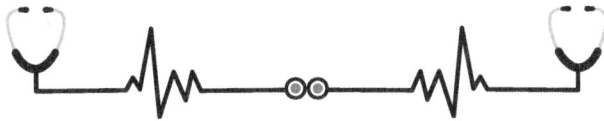

THE JOURNEY WE TOOK TOGETHER

If you're reading this chapter, I want you to pause - just for a moment - and acknowledge something: You stayed. You showed up. You turned each page. You gave yourself time, space, and grace. You said: I matter enough to heal. And I want you to know - that's everything.

Because healing doesn't always feel like fireworks. It's often quiet. Subtle. Slow. It's choosing to breathe when your thoughts race. It's reaching out when it feels safer to disappear. It's letting yourself feel when numbness was once your armor.

WHAT SHIFTED IN ME

When I first felt the heaviness of burnout, I thought I was the problem. I thought I was weak. Lazy. Dramatic. But I wasn't broken -
I was burdened. I didn't need to be fixed -
I needed to be seen. By others. And most importantly, by myself.

So I turned inward. And what I found wasn't just pain... I found a part of me that had been waiting to be loved back to life.

Through every breath, every pause, every reset... I changed.

I became softer - but not weaker.
Slower - but more intentional.
Quieter - but more connected.

I became my own caregiver.
And now - I want that for you, too.

YOU DON'T GO BACK - YOU GROW FORWARD

You may never be the person you were before the burnout, the depression, the loss, the dark days.

That's not failure.
That's evolution.

You are becoming someone new - someone stronger in spirit, softer in soul, clearer in purpose.

The shift in you is not loud.
But it's real.
And it matters.

WHAT YOU CAN CARRY FORWARD

If this book has offered you anything -
a moment of calm, a tool, a truth - hold onto it.

You don't need to remember every chapter.

Just remember:

- You are not alone.
- You are not your darkest thought.
- You are not behind.
- You are not broken.
- You are already healing.

One deep breath at a time.
One thought at a time.
One gentle moment at a time.

YOUR LIGHT IS STILL HERE

You are the light after shift.
You are the soft glow in the quiet night.
You are a caregiver, a soul-healer, a heart
with resilience written in its rhythm.
So keep going. Keep choosing you.
Keep coming home to yourself.

SELF-CARE TEMPLATE #1:
DAILY SELF-COMPASSION CHECK-IN

Today's Date: _____

1. One word to describe how I feel today:

2. Body Scan – What sensations do I notice right now?
(Example: tension, calm, tight chest, tired feet)

3. Emotions I am experiencing:
- Calm
- Anxious
- Overwhelmed
- Sad
- Grateful
- Numb
- Other: _____

4. What is one need I have today?
(Physical, emotional, spiritual)

5. What can I do in the next 10 minutes to support myself?

6. One gentle thing I can say to myself today:

"_____"

SELF-CARE TEMPLATE #2:
WEEKLY BOUNDARY + ENERGY CHECK

This Week's Theme:
(What I want to focus on emotionally, mentally, or physically)

What Drains Me:
List 3 things that deplete your energy (people, tasks, habits).

-
-
-

What Nourishes Me:
List 3 things that replenish you.

-
-
-

Boundary I need to set this week:

One thing I will say "no" to this week:

One thing I will say "yes" to that supports my well-being:

SELF-CARE TEMPLATE #3:
MY EMOTIONAL
FIRST AID PLAN

This is your go-to guide when emotions feel overwhelming. Complete it now so it's ready when needed. When I feel overwhelmed or triggered, I will...

1. Grounding Tool I Will Use:
(Ex: deep breathing, 5-4-3-2-1 senses, hold ice cube)

2. Calming Statement I'll Repeat:

"_____"

3. Safe Space I Can Go To:
(Room, nature, car, bath, etc.)

4. Support Person I Can Reach Out To:

Name: _____

Phone/Text: _____

5. One Kind Reminder:

"Feelings pass. I am not alone. I don't have to fix it all right now."

SELF-CARE TEMPLATE #4:
CREATE YOUR SELF-SOOTHE KIT

Fill this out and keep it somewhere visible.

What comforts me when I feel down:

- Smell: _____
(Ex: lavender, coffee, lotion)

- Sound: _____
(Ex: calming playlist, rain sounds)

- Sight: _____
(Ex: candles, nature photos)

- Touch: _____
(Ex: soft blanket, warm shower)

- Taste: _____
(Ex: tea, favorite snack)

One sentence that reminds me I am safe:

"_____"

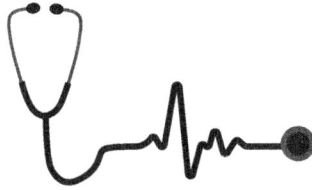

AFFIRMATIONS

*Words to whisper when
the world feels heavy.
Truths to anchor you when
you forget your own.*

AFFIRMATION
DAY 1

"
I deserve the same compassion
I offer to everyone else.
"

AFFIRMATION
DAY 2

"
It's okay to pause.
The world won't fall apart if I rest.
"

AFFIRMATION
DAY 3

> "I am not my exhaustion -
> I am a human who's been
> carrying too much."

AFFIRMATION
DAY 4

"
Healing isn't selfish.
It's sacred.
"

AFFIRMATION
DAY 5

"
My softness is not a weakness.
It's a form of courage.
"

AFFIRMATION
DAY 6

"

*I don't need to fix everything.
I just need to feel this moment.*

"

AFFIRMATION
DAY 7

"
I am allowed to need help.
Even strong people need support.
"

AFFIRMATION
DAY 8

"
I can hold space for
others and myself.
"

AFFIRMATION
DAY 9

> *Every breath I take is proof that I am still here, still becoming.*

AFFIRMATION
DAY 10

"
I choose peace,
even if my mind resists it.
"

AFFIRMATION
DAY 11

I am not behind.
I am right on time
for my own healing.

AFFIRMATION
DAY 12

"
I don't need to do
more to be enough.
I already am.
"

AFFIRMATION
DAY 13

> *I am learning how to
> show up for myself.
> And that's enough for today.*

AFFIRMATION
DAY 14

"
It is safe to slow down.
The shift is over.
"

AFFIRMATION
DAY 15

> " I release the pressure
> to be perfect.
> I welcome being real. "

AFFIRMATION
DAY 16

My body is not a machine - it's a miracle in motion.

AFFIRMATION
DAY 17

"

Even when I feel lost,
I am still worthy of love.

„

AFFIRMATION
DAY 18

"

I carry wisdom in my hands and tenderness in my heart.

"

AFFIRMATION
DAY 19

"
I don't have to hold it
all together to be strong.
"

AFFIRMATION
DAY 20

"
I am not alone in this.
Others are healing too.
"

AFFIRMATION
DAY 21

" Rest is not quitting.
Rest is part of the work. "

AFFIRMATION
DAY 22

"
My presence is enough.
My existence is enough.
"

AFFIRMATION
DAY 23

" I can start again at any moment.
Even now. "

AFFIRMATION
DAY 24

"
I trust that my emotions are
messengers - not enemies.
"

AFFIRMATION
DAY 25

"
I honor the version of me that
kept going through the storm.
"

AFFIRMATION
DAY 26

> I am healing in ways
> I can't always see.

AFFIRMATION
DAY 27

"
I release the guilt for what I couldn't do and embrace what I can.
"

AFFIRMATION
DAY 28

"
My worth is not tied to
my productivity.
"

AFFIRMATION
DAY 29

" *I choose to meet myself with gentleness, not judgment.* "

AFFIRMATION
DAY 30

Light still lives in me – and I am learning how to let it shine again.

MY HOPE FILE

A place to keep the light when life feels dim. This page is for the reminders, the moments, the voices, and the truths that help you hold on - especially when you feel like letting go. Fill it with anything that helps you believe again.

1. Messages I want to remember when I feel low: (Kind words, affirmations, or notes to yourself)

....

....

....

....

....

....

....

....

....

....

2. People who make me feel safe and seen:
(List names or initials)

....

....

....

....

....

....

....

....

....

....

3. Moments I felt strong, peaceful, or proud:
(Even the small ones count)

....

....

....

....

....

....

....

....

....

....

4. Quotes or verses that lift me:
(Add your favorites - spiritual, inspiring,
or comforting)

....

....

....

....

....

....

....

....

....

....

5. My reasons to keep going:
(What or who gives your life meaning)

....

....

....

....

....

....

....

....

....

....

MY HOPE FILE

Keep this page close. Return to it often. Add to it freely. Your hope is real - even if it feels small. And every word you write here is a light you'll be able to return to, again and again.

RESOURCES LIST

PROFESSIONAL TOOLS TO SUPPORT
YOUR MENTAL HEALTH JOURNEY.

These tools are not a substitute for clinical care - but they are powerful companions on your path to healing, support, and self-connection.

MENTAL HEALTH HOTLINES & TEXT LINES

- **988 Suicide & Crisis Lifeline (USA)**
Call or text 988 - Free, confidential support 24/7 for anyone in emotional distress.

- **Crisis Text Line (USA, UK, Canada)**
Text HELLO to 741741 - Trained crisis counselors available 24/7.

- **National Alliance on Mental Illness**
(NAMI Helpline) 1-800-950-NAMI (6264) or text "NAMI" to 741741. Info, education, and support for mental illness and caregiver burnout.

- **Nurse Suicide Prevention Hotline (USA)**
Call or text 1-800-662-HELP (4357)
- Available 24/7, anonymous support.

THERAPY & TELEHEALTH PLATFORMS

- BetterHelp - Affordable online therapy with licensed counselors. (www.betterhelp.com)

- Talkspace - Text and video therapy for individuals, couples, and teens. (www.talkspace.com)

- Headway - Find therapists who take your insurance in the U.S. (www.headway.co)

- Open Path Collective - Sliding scale therapy options for low-income individuals. (www.openpathcollective.org)

- Inclusive Therapists - Focused on intersectional, trauma-informed care for all identities. (www.inclusivetherapists.com)

MOBILE APPS FOR MENTAL WELLNESS

- Insight Timer - Free meditations, sleep sounds, breathing tools

- Calm - Meditation, sleep stories, and gentle stress relief

- Headspace - Guided mindfulness and stress reduction

- Moodpath / MindDoc - Mood tracking and journal prompts with clinical insights

- Sanvello - Anxiety and depression management tools based on CBT (Cognitive-Behavioral Therapy)

- Shine - Support for BIPOC mental health with daily self-care support

- I Am - Affirmation app with powerful daily reminders for self-worth

NURSE & CAREGIVER SUPPORT GROUPS

- **The Resilient Nurse Project** - Support for nurses navigating burnout

- **Sonsiel (Society of Nurse Scientists, Innovators, Entrepreneurs & Leaders)** - Resources for nurses' personal and professional growth

- **NurseGrid Community** - Peer connection through scheduling app and forums

- **Facebook Groups:**
  "Nurse Mental Health Support"
  "Compassion Fatigue & Burnout Prevention for Nurses"
  "Healing Nurses Circle"

DISCLAIMER: NO SPONSORSHIP OR AFFILIATION

The resources listed in this book are shared purely to support your mental health journey. I am not sponsored, paid, or affiliated with any of the organizations, apps, or platforms mentioned.

These recommendations are based on personal use, professional insight, and positive feedback from trusted peers in healthcare and mental wellness.

Please explore them based on your own needs, and consult with a licensed professional for clinical guidance.

MY REFLECTION SPACE

This is your space.
A page to pause, breathe,
and reflect. Write freely.
There are no rules here –
only honesty, healing, and the
gentle unfolding of your heart.

MY REFLECTION SPACE

....

....

....

....

....

....

....

....

....

....

....

MY REFLECTION SPACE

....

....

....

....

....

....

....

....

....

....

....

MY REFLECTION SPACE

....

....

....

....

....

....

....

....

....

....

....

MY REFLECTION SPACE

....

....

....

....

....

....

....

....

....

....

....

MY REFLECTION SPACE

MY REFLECTION SPACE

MY REFLECTION SPACE

....

....

....

....

....

....

....

....

....

....

....

MY REFLECTION SPACE

....

....

....

....

....

....

....

....

....

....

....

MY REFLECTION SPACE

....

....

....

....

....

....

....

....

....

....

....

....

MY REFLECTION SPACE

....

....

....

....

....

....

....

....

....

....

....

MY GRATITUDE LIST

*Amid burnout, stress, or
emotional heaviness, gratitude
can be a powerful anchor.
Use this page to list the moments,
people, or things you are
thankful for - big or small.
Let this be a gentle reminder
that light still exists,
even on the hard days.*

MY GRATITUDE LIST

....

....

....

....

....

....

....

....

....

....

....

MY GRATITUDE LIST

....

....

....

....

....

....

....

....

....

....

....

MY GRATITUDE LIST

···

···

···

···

···

···

···

···

···

···

···

MY GRATITUDE LIST

....

....

....

....

....

....

....

....

....

....

....

MY GRATITUDE LIST

....

....

....

....

....

....

....

....

....

....

....

MY GRATITUDE LIST

....

....

....

....

....

....

....

....

....

....

....

MY GRATITUDE LIST

....

....

....

....

....

....

....

....

....

....

MY GRATITUDE LIST

MY GRATITUDE LIST

....

....

....

....

....

....

....

....

....

....

....

MY GRATITUDE LIST

....

....

....

....

....

....

....

....

....

....

....

Prayers for you...

A PRAYER FOR HEALING FROM BURNOUT AND DEPRESSION

Dear God,

I come to You weary and worn out.
The weight I carry feels too heavy, and joy feels far away. I've poured out so much that I've forgotten what it means to feel whole.

But today, I give You the broken pieces – my fatigue, my numbness, my sadness, my fading fire. Heal me, not just in body, but in spirit. Restore what burnout has taken, and remind me that I'm loved not for what I do, but for who I am.

Fill my empty spaces with Your peace.
Light up the dark corners where hope has dimmed. Teach me true rest in You.
I surrender what I'm trying to hold together and receive Your grace instead.

Thank You for seeing me, loving me, and never giving up on me. Even when healing is slow, I choose to believe it's coming.

Amen.

A PRAYER BEFORE SHIFT

Dear God,

As I start this shift, I open my heart to You. Fill me with peace, calm my mind, and trade my worries for trust.

Give me strength for what's ahead, patience in the hard moments, and compassion that endures. Guard my mind, soften my heart, and protect my spirit from burnout.

Remind me that I'm never alone – You are with me in every breath. Let me bring light, healing, and kindness to those I meet. And when the day is done, help me release the weight, find rest, and remember:

I was enough.

Amen.

A NIGHTTIME PRAYER AFTER SHIFT

Dear God,

The shift is over, and I bring You all of it – the good, the hard, and the uncertain.
I gave what I could, and now I let the rest go.

Help me release what I couldn't fix, the words left unsaid, and the weight I carried in silence. Wrap me in Your peace. Quiet my mind, calm my body, and let my soul rest in You.

Restore what's drained, heal what's heavy, and remind me: I don't have to hold it all – because You are holding me.

Thank You for today's strength and tomorrow's grace.

Tonight, I rest. And that is enough.

Amen.

Thank You ♥

Dear Readers,

To you –
The one holding this book with tired hands, searching for peace in quiet moments, giving so much and wondering if there's anything left for you – this is for you. I don't have all the answers, but I've been where you are. I know the quiet weight you carry and the strength it takes to keep going when you're running on empty. You are not alone. Healing isn't a race – it's found in small breaths, soft pauses, and tiny sparks of hope. If this book brings even a moment of peace or reminds you that you matter, then it's done what I hoped it would.

Thank you for letting me walk with you.
Keep rising gently.
Your light is still here – brighter than you know.

With Care,

Zyra Ann Boniel

ABOUT THE AUTHOR

Zyra Ann Boniel

A proud mother, devoted wife, compassionate nurse, passionate author of children's books, and a purpose-driven author focused on healing bodies, and hearts and inspiring hope. She has been working as a nurse since 2008, caring deeply for the well-being of others – both at the bedside and now through the written word.

What began as a career in healing the body has grown into a passion for healing the heart and mind through words. As a self-help and wellness book author, she offers comfort, encouragement, and tools for mental, emotional, and spiritual healing.

Her mission is to leave a legacy – not only for her family but for readers around the world – by writing books that uplift, restore, and promote lasting well-being.

Zyra believes that every story told with purpose can change a life. And through her work, she hopes to light the way for others to rediscover hope, health, and healing.

NOTES:

NOTES:

NOTES:

NOTES:

NOTES:

NOTES:

NOTES:

NOTES:

NOTES:

NOTES:

NOTES:

NOTES:

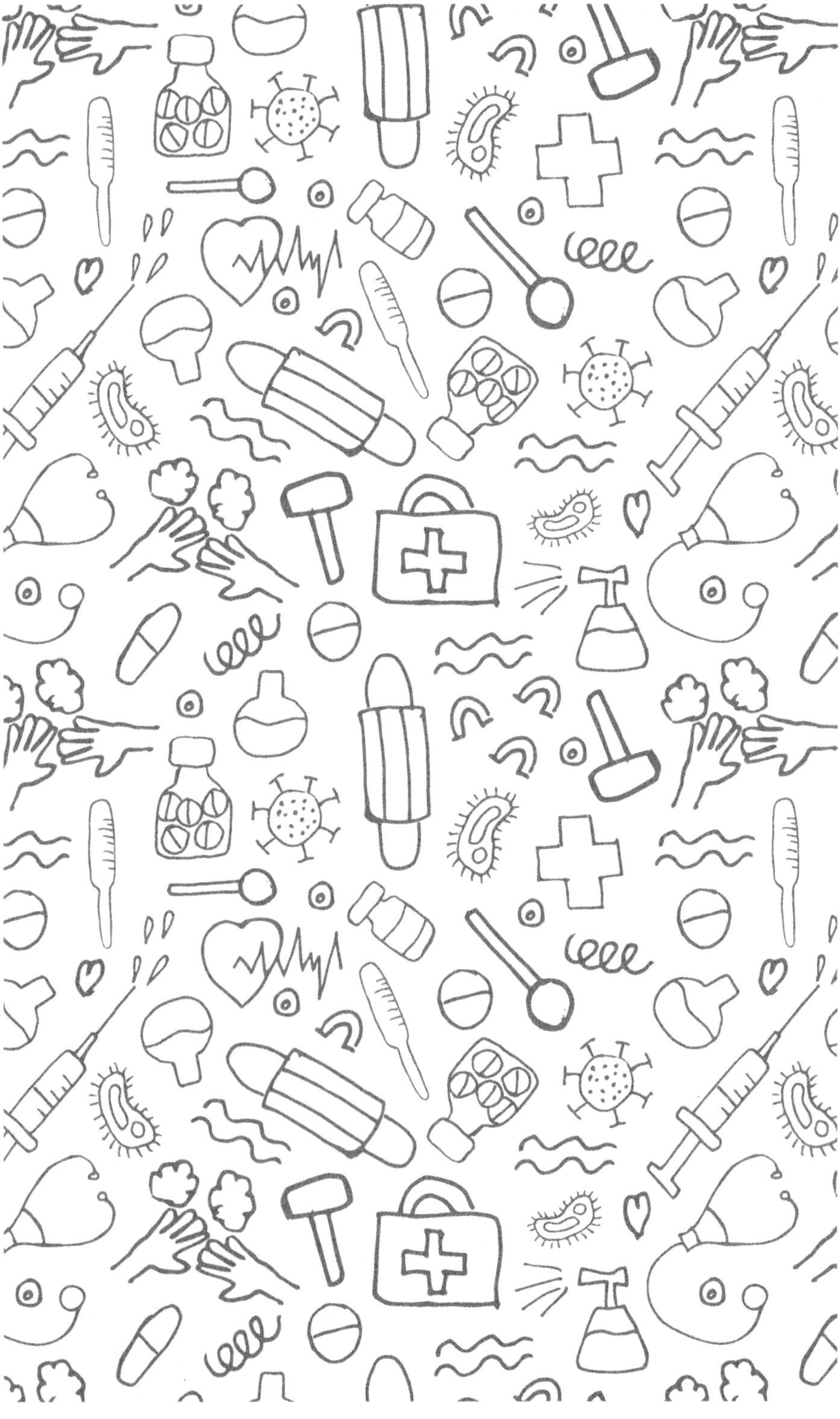